7 SECRETS THAT TRANSFORM YOU FROM MOM TO MOMPRENEUR

BECOME A BOSS WHILE RUNNING A FAMILY

KARISHMA GUPTA & ARJUN GUPTA

Worldwide Published by
Pendown Press

PENDOWN PRESS LLP
An ISO 9001 & ISO 14001 Certified Co.,
Regd. Office: 3767A, Kanhaiya Nagar,
Tri Nagar, Delhi-110035
Ph.: 8130886000, 9650072927, 8595249536
E-mail: info@pendownpress.com
Branch Office: 1A/2A, 20, Hari Sadan, Ansari Road,
Daryaganj, New Delhi-110002
Ph.: 011-45794768
Website: PendownPress.com

First Edition: 2023
Price: ₹599/-
ISBN: 978-93-5554-662-3

Layout and Cover Designed by Pendown Graphics Team
Printed and Bound in India by Thomson Press India Ltd.

*This book is dedicated to those
who dared to dream and had the
courage to pursue it.*

यत्र नार्यस्तु पूज्यन्ते रमन्ते तत्र देवता:।
यत्रेतास्तु न पूज्यन्ते सर्वास्तत्राफला क्रिया:।।

भावार्थ

जिस कुल में स्त्रियों की पूजा होती है, सत्कार होता है,
उस कुल में दिव्यगुण, दिव्यभोग और उत्तम संतान होते हैं
और जिस कुल में स्त्रियों की पूजा नहीं होती,
वहां उनकी सब क्रिया निष्फल है!

Meaning

*Where women are honoured, divinity
blossoms there, and where ever women are
dishonoured, all action no matter How
noble it may be, remains unfruitful!*

Contents

Introduction

We would like to start this book with a story. A story that you may have heard before, but the way we will take this one, will shape your future.

Once upon a time, in a small town in Uttar Pradesh, there lived a woman named Rekha. She was a mother and a housewife, facing many problems at home, especially concerning money. The family's financial troubles often left her feeling helpless.

But what made things even more challenging for Rekha was her struggle with stammering. Whenever she had to speak in front of outsiders, her words would get tangled in her throat, making her feel embarrassed. She wished she could communicate more confidently, but it seemed like an impossible dream.

One day, while browsing the internet, Rekha stumbled upon a passive income network. It promised a way to earn money without a traditional job, and Rekha decided to give it a try. She started investing her time and effort into this new opportunity, and slowly but surely, things began to change.

As Rekha started earning money from her passive income network, she became more independent. She no longer had to beg her husband for money to manage household expenses. This newfound financial freedom brought respect from her husband, who now admired her determination and hard work.

Rekha's children noticed the change in their mother as well. They began to love her even more because she could provide for them without worry. Rekha could now go shopping on her own, buy things for her family, and even save for the future.

Her achievements didn't stop there. Rekha's confidence grew day by day. She started participating in community events and meetings related to her passive income network. Initially, she struggled with her stammering, but with time and practice, she spoke more fluently in front of hundreds of people. Her newfound confidence earned her recognition in her society and at home.

Rekha's story showed everyone in the town that with determination and the right opportunity, anyone could transform their life. She went from being a financially struggling housewife who stammered in front of outsiders to a confident and independent woman, respected by her family and society.

So, remember Rekha's story. It teaches us that change is possible, and with perseverance, we can shape our own future.

Similar stories exist in most households in India, and we are here so that you can experience a similar radical shift, just as Rekha did in her life.

Jahaan Chah hai, vahaan Raah hai!!!
All you need is Junoon (Passion)!!

Have you ever wished you didn't have to ask for money?

Have you ever felt trapped, unable to control your finances because you depend on someone else?

Do you hate begging for money from your spouse every time?

Has your self-confidence suffered at Home?

If any of these concerns bothers you, there's good news. There are opportunities available that allow you to work from home and take steps toward financial freedom.

The purpose of this book is to guide you in unlocking your potential for financial abundance.

I aim to help you develop a healthier attitude toward money.

If this is what you desire, I've created a simple SEVEN-STEP PLAN just for you.

What is the purpose behind this step?

Because moms deserve to fulfil their dreams, and I want you to feel the same way.

But you only feel like that when you start to change this relationship that we have had with money for such a long time.

We, Arjun Gupta and Karishma Gupta, authors of this book, are life coaches and mindset enhancers.

We are helping thousands of women across the country in gaining self-respect along with financial independence. We also aim to shape the identity they have been looking for.

If any of this resonates with you, I want you to know that you will also learn how to gain financial independence and how to get the support of your husband and everyone around you whether it's your mother-in-law, parents, or whoever is currently not supporting you.

You will also become a proud mother, wife & daughter.

If any of this inspires you and you feel like you want to align your life again with the flow of what it should be, then this book is for you. It can help you overcome all your challenges and achieve everything you have ever dreamt of.

Why This Book?

What a coward lady she is!

She cannot do anything!

She cannot even look after her house!

She cannot even manage her work!

She cannot go outside to buy groceries!

She can't even take care of her husband!

She can't even look after kids properly!

She cannot cook meals!

She does nothing at all!

She fails to meet her husband's needs.

Do these phrases sound familiar to you??

Unfortunately, these sentences are all too familiar to many of us. Whether it's about our appearance, abilities, or personal choices, such words can leave a lasting impact. It's disheartening to hear such remarks, but it's essential to remember that they don't define our worth or capabilities. We should strive to rise above these discouragements and stay true to ourselves, recognizing our strengths and embracing our uniqueness. Let us not be disheartened by the words of others but, instead, find the courage to pursue our dreams and live life on our terms. These are certain remarks many of you must have come across. If you, too, are familiar with them, then please go ahead:

If somewhere deep down in your heart and mind, you feel that your confidence has been laid down, and yet you have the determination to work. Unfortunately, you may not be willing to take that step. Your idea of earning extra income may have been hindered due to being stuck somewhere. You could not find the path on how to grow and lead a successful life for good health and wealth.

This book is tailor-made for highly ambitious mothers, homemakers, and anyone with unfulfilled dreams due to various responsibilities - those who crave to achieve their aspirations and attain financial independence. It's time to break free from limitations, embrace your desires, and embark on a path that leads to the fulfilment of your dreams. Let's empower you to live the life you've always envisioned. Together, we can make those dreams a vibrant reality!

This book is for all those people who want to earn money, respect, and become financially independent. Everyone has certain dreams, but due to several responsibilities, their dreams get deferred. They are unable to sustain and live their dreams. So, to give those dreams a LIFE, we are here for you!

Hum Saath Saath Hain!!
(We Are Together!!)

Whom This Book For?

If you want to create your own business and earn extra income of more than Rs. 25,000 per month within 6 months, you're in the right place. Due to growing family responsibilities, it is difficult for women to focus on financial independence, which is why online opportunities have been created. Even you would be surprised to know how Mrs. Sriharia, a housewife, increased her family income to Rs.60,000/month from her home.

Finding the right balance between making money and handling family life is a universal aspiration. Everyone desires to support themselves and their loved ones comfortably. Join the ranks of millions of women who have already embraced this business opportunity. With this proven system, you can embark on a rewarding journey towards financial prosperity while still prioritizing your family's well-being. It's time to seize the chance to attain both professional and personal fulfilment. Let us learn more about this path to success, where you can strike the perfect balance between earning money and cherishing precious moments with your family. Together, we can unlock a future filled with abundance and happiness.

So, use the fail-proof system and start to earn like millions of other women who are benefiting from this business.

This book is for all those people who:

- Want to live an independent life

- Want to open luxurious opportunities for themselves

- Want to work from home

- Want to make their own financial decisions

- Want to have their own identity

- Want to be an ambitious women

Living an independent life is a dream for everyone. Independence can mean different things to different individuals, but it often involves having the freedom to make choices, achieve personal goals, and live life on their own terms. Also, opening up luxurious opportunities for oneself is an aspiration for many.

The desire to work from home has seen an increase in demand. Working from home offers countless advantages. We can create our own schedules, eliminate stress, and establish a comfortable workspace. This is the best option for all the ladies who want to manage household responsibilities along with their kids and earn money beforehand. It also helps in achieving a work-life balance.

Watching housewives beg for money is tormenting for women these days. Are you tired of begging for money from your husband or your in-laws? Women crave the ability to make their financial decisions by themselves. Dominance has played a major role, whether it's from husbands or from in-laws. Women want to have their own identity.

About Book

All educated women want to present their values and thoughts in front of someone so that they don't get deferred. The tide is turning as women increasingly strive to break free from these constraints. They define themselves on their own terms and express their passions, talents, and dreams.

So, if a woman is ambitious enough to earn and fulfil her dreams and needs to put her thoughts, ideas, and values before anything, then this book is a must for her.

This book contains a step-by-step framework that will help Mompreneurs and Homepreneurs to nurture leaders in their teams.

This book serves as an invaluable resource for cultivating leadership within their teams. In today's business landscape, the role of women in entrepreneurship has never been more prominent, and this book is designed to harness their potential. By following this book, Mompreneurs and Homepreneurs can gain the insights and strategies necessary to foster leadership qualities in their team members.

Whether it's effective communication, promoting teamwork, or engaging in a sense of responsibility, this book provides a roadmap for success. As women face the challenge of balancing business and home responsibilities, with the help of this book, they can become the emerging leaders of tomorrow.

A woman has the dual responsibility of managing both home and work, and we aim to make them independent. Our book is the right business tool that will help them grow exponentially.

Circle of Income

Everyone has dreams. One might want their kids to get a good education; another may dream of owning a luxury car, and someone wants a lavish family world tour. Only a few focus on having considerable savings.

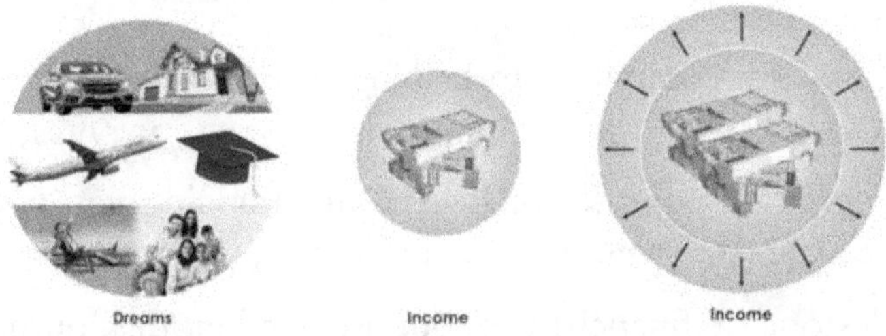

In the above diagram, you can see two circles. One is the circle of dreams, and the other is the circle of income. Our circle of dreams is very big. However, to fulfil our goals, we must take care of our circle of INCOME. We should be aware that to achieve our dreams, the only way is to make our circle of INCOME big enough to cover the circle of our DREAMS.

This book is for those who want to work as per their flexibility and on their own terms. Work flexibility means working when you want to work, offering the freedom to choose working hours and patterns. If someone wants to work more on certain days, they can choose to do so and work less on days when they don't want to.

Work-life flexibility is a key advantage of direct selling, making it an attractive career choice for many individuals who seek a balance between professional and personal life.

Also, if you want to secure your financial future and make your own financial decisions, if you want to be the boss of your own, then you shouldn't skip this part.

We want to start with a big promise. Our big promise is that "After reading this book, you will have a clear path on How You Can Earn up to Rs.25,000 per month or even more within the next 6 months from the comfort of your home."

Yes, we are committed to helping you achieve the target of earning a passive monthly income of up to Rs.25,000 or more in the next six months. We believe in providing you with the TOOLS, KNOWLEDGE, and SUPPORT necessary to reach this milestone of financial freedom. Remember, this journey will require dedication, consistent effort, and a willingness to learn and grow. This book will serve as your roadmap, and we're here to assist you every step of the way toward your financial success.

India has experienced rapid growth and development over the years, creating immense opportunities for individuals to achieve their dreams. We all know that India is growing; our economy is among the fastest-growing economies in the world. We are racing to become the 3rd largest economy. But does this satisfactorily reflect your income so well? Are we financially independent and growing as individuals?

In the past 25 years, we have witnessed the American Dream unfold in the USA, and now it's time for us to pursue the Indian

Dream. Remarkably, the landscape has transformed, as even college students, teenagers, and homemakers are attaining financial success. Every week, we witness the emergence of new Lakhpatis and Crorepatis in India.

With Auretics Business Opportunity, we aspire to provide you with a pathway towards becoming a Lakhpati. Let's embark on this journey together and unlock the potential to achieve financial prosperity on your own terms.

Within the next pages, you will discover a few important learnings:

- The potential of the Direct Selling Industry
- How to find the Right Company to start with
- Why become a Digital Network Marketer
- Rocket Marketeer Framework (7 Steps)
- How to make these steps EASY
- How to fulfil all your Dreams

About Us

Before we move forward, we would like to introduce you to our group.

Our mother company is PharmaSynth Formulations Limited, which has been serving the nation since 1984. We have been conferred with various National and International prestigious awards for quality, productivity, and fair business practices; a few of them worth mentioning are:

1. "Excellence Award" and Udyog Ratna by IES, New Delhi.

2. "International Star Award for Quality in Gold category" by BID at their Geneva convention in the year 2007.

3. "National Award-2007" for Quality by the Ministry of MSME, Govt. of India, presented by Hon'ble Prime Minister Dr. Manmohan Singh.

4. "Special Recognition Award" by the Government of Uttarakhand.

5. "MSME award" by National Productivity Council of India, Ministry of Commerce & Industry, Govt. of India for excellence in productivity in 2010.

6. "Fair Business Practices Award" by the Council of corporate code of conduct, Mumbai.

7. A national award with international repute, "Rajiv Gandhi National Quality Award-2011" by BIS, Ministry of Consumer Affairs, Govt. of India.

The most prestigious award was the National Award 2007 – given by our then Honourable Prime Minister "Mr Manmohan Singh Ji". There are various social and patriotic activities run by our company, such as "Beti Bachao Abhiyan", "Mission Ganga Safai Abhiyan", "Save Abhiyan, Save Earth", and so on.

After having a strong hold in the traditional allopathic market (illness industry), we have started another division: Auretics Limited.

Auretics is a direct-selling company where we have researched and developed various wellness supplements, fitness & personal care products. Catering in the direct selling industry, we provide a passive income opportunity for everyone.

We have been covered by various news agencies like The Pioneer, Hindustan, Daikin Bhaskar, Dainik Jagran, Hindustan Times, Hello Entrepreneurs, Hindustan, etc.

Testimonials

We have got support from various individuals, who have partnered with us to achieve their personal and professional goals. Some of them are here:

"No other Direct Selling Company has spray-based products like "SugarRodhi" for sugar management. That's making it peculiar. Also, the customer care service is instantly available to the customers which is very helpful."

~Mr. Deepa Thakkar
(Independent Auretics Distributor)

"Auretics has an amazing Business plan. I am pleased with Consistent Retailer's Income (CRI). "Facewash is an amazing product" as it gives results within 2-3 months. The pricing looks very reasonable and the packaging also looks appealing.

~Mrs. Nida Fatima
(Independent Auretics Distributor)

"The product" "SugarRodhi" has given tremendous results. Many people are using SugarRodhi. This product is more than 90% effective. In fact," Speedex Joint Support" is also an effective remedy for joint pain."

~Mr. Rajesh Yadav
(Independent Auretics Distributor)

"People are leaving their private jobs for Auretics as it is giving earning opportunities to people. The product "Multiammrit" is very remarkable and showed effective results in people who are using it. Also, I am very much satisfied with the "Customer Care Operations" instant availability."

~Ms. Pushpa Negi
(Independent Auretics Distributor)

"SugarRodhi is very effective in controlling Diabetes of the patients. Auretics provides marvellous schemes to the customers. The benefits of "Consistent Retailer's Income" are leaving people astonished and making it distinguishable from other companies."

~Mr. Nilmoni Dey
(Independent Auretics Distributor)

"I am very much happy with the quality of juices such as "Sea Buckthorn", "Aloe vera", "Garcinia". Also, the cost is affordable to me as compared with the market prices. No other direct-selling company is giving products at such affordable rates."

-Mrs. Bromi Panchal
(Independent Auretics Distributor)

"I believe that" "SugarRodhi", and "PressureRodhi" are the backbone of the company. No other company spray-based products as we have here in Auretics."

~Mr. Dharmendra Kumar Sharma
(Independent Auretics Distributor)

"For me, "CareVed Herbal Eye Drop" is like an elixir to the eyes. It provides me with the deepest relaxation. Also, I used "Acno-Vanish" and "Cream" and the result is out shown. I am very happy and satisfied with the Pricing and Quality of the products."

~Mr. Arjun Paramar
(Independent Auretics Distributor)

"Pricing and Products quality of Auretics Products is at its best. I should have joined this amazing opportunity earlier that could have brightened my future earlier. It's an amazing platform to be the king of your own business."

~Mr. Dashrath Thakur
(Independent Auretics Distributor)

"I love Skin Care products such as "AcnoVanish". It has affordable pricing. I want to fulfil my dreams with the platform of Auretics as I am highly confident about the trust of the company.

~Mrs. Neelam Vaghela
(Independent Auretics Distributor)

"I have joined Auretics from the start and I am sure that a lot of people are going to become diamonds in my network and we all will succeed together as a team.

~Mr. Ashis Das
(Independent Auretics Distributor)

"Auretics is like a dream company for me. I have used many supplements from Auretics and my team and customer base love them due to fit results and good quality.

Products are 5 stars, management is stars, and the company has spread its wings nationally and internationally so it is aa lsoa star. The compensation plan is also 5 stars. I don't plan to go anywhere else."

~Mr. Bisweswar Bag
(Independent Auretics Distributor)

"I have recently joined Auretics and I like Auretics Spray based Products. I have used it myself and my BP was normalised within a few days and I am very satisfied."

~Mr. Prabir Chakraborty
(Independent Auretics Distributor)

"I was facing sugar management issues and had irritation in my feet. I have got good results with SugarRodhi and my sugar is under control. I have used MultiAmmrit also and my health is improved. I see good earnings in the future with Auretics Business.

~Mr. Harish Natchlani
(Independent Auretics Distributor)

Till this part, we aim to grow mentally, physically, and emotionally to become financially independent. So, my dear friends, when I say "OWN YOUR LIFE," what does it mean?

Owning your life means that when you subtract the working time and daily chores, most people are hardly left with less than

2 hours to exercise their hobbies or spend time doing what they love to do. We have discovered a way that allows a person to learn how to **"OWN THEIR LIFE"** by building a home-based business. We have an established system for doing so that will help you start and scale your business.

It doesn't require selling…

It won't take much of your time…

If you are interested, you're on the right path.

In short, it is *"Mai Rani Hu Apni Zindagi Ki"*. So, if you want to be the *"Rani"* of your own *Zindagi,*

Go ahead and know the secret: shhhhhhh…

Chapter 1

The potential
of the Direct Selling Industry

What's DIRECT SELLING: Yes, everyone knows, it's Multi-Level Marketing.

Let me define it:

Multi: Multi means more than one

Level: Level refers to the generations

Marketing: Moving a product from the manufacturer to the consumer.

In short, DIRECT SELLING is a method of marketing where you earn from the product you share and also from the products your referrals share.

Traditional Business Model vs Direct Selling Model

Let's discuss the Traditional Business Model vs the Direct Selling Model.

What is the Traditional Business Model?

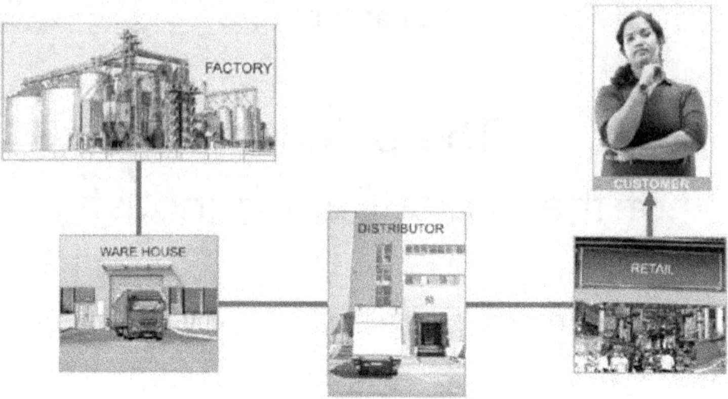

In a traditional business, a company makes products and sells them through stores. The company spends a lot on advertising and pays employees to sell the products. The traditional business model involves multiple channels, wherein after the product gets manufactured, it goes to the WAREHOUSE, then to the DISTRIBUTOR. There are various sub-categories of distributors, ranging from super distributors or sub-distributors to the RETAILER and finally to the CUSTOMER. Now, the product passes through various middlemen, who charge their fees and commission on the product, which increases the price of the product. The customer buys directly from the store, and there is usually no one-on-one interaction between you and the seller.

What is the Direct Selling Model?

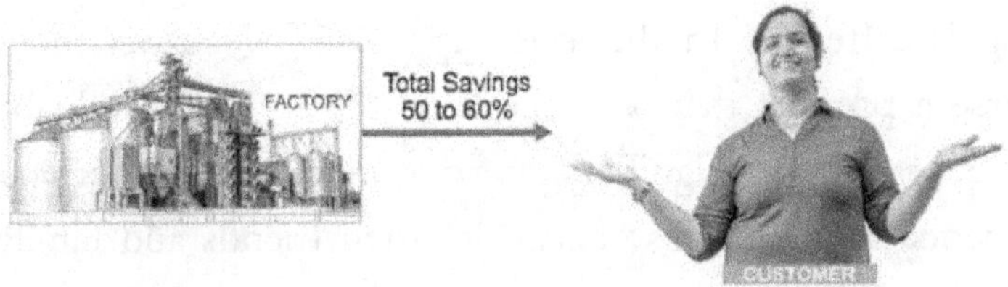

In direct selling, a company sells products directly through independent representatives or distributors, resulting in savings of around 50-60%. This happens due to the absence of middlemen, and these savings are passed on to the representatives. These representatives often work from home and directly sell products to customers. They might also recruit others to become company representatives and earn a commission from their sales. This model often involves more personal interactions, like meetings, training sessions, seminars, or demonstrations, where you can see and try the products.

In a nutshell, the main difference lies in how the products are sold. In traditional business, it's usually through stores or websites, while in direct selling, it's through independent representatives who often adopt a more personal approach.

Direct selling ka matlab more engaging relationships with customers.

Keep in mind:

"We are not in the Business of Selling,
We are in the Business of Sharing."

~Arjun Gupta

Traditional selling involves "calling strangers and trying to sell them something they neither need nor want." But direct selling is different. In this sales approach, we experience and endorse a product that we believe in. If we find it valuable or believe it can make a significant impact, we then share our positive experience with our close network, often friends and family.

In the direct selling Network Model, a noteworthy 74% of participants are women, underscoring the significant presence and active engagement of women in this industry, while the remaining 26% are men.

The direct selling network provides a unique platform for women to embrace entrepreneurship, achieve financial independence, and excel in their chosen paths. It offers equal opportunities for success and growth to individuals irrespective of gender. As we celebrate the remarkable contributions of women in Direct Selling, we also encourage and welcome the participation of men. It's a place where everyone can do their best and succeed together.

Undoubtedly, this stands as a women-dominated industry. There are several reasons why network marketing has attracted a significant number of women. First, network marketing offers flexibility, allowing individuals to work from home and set their schedules.

We take pride in the expansion of the direct selling industry, evident in both its market size and the number of active participants. Notably, there has been a remarkable overall growth rate of approximately 18%. What's even more astonishing is the increase in active individuals within the Direct Selling Industry when compared to previous years. This surge is attributed to technological advancements and improved customer connectivity. Here's an interesting fact: a lot of people are buying the wellness and cosmetics sectors. These are things that help people take care of themselves and feel good.

Wellness products are designed to promote health and overall well-being. These include weight management products, fitness products, and certain natural remedies.

Cosmetics include skin care, makeup, and personal products. We emphasize the quality & effectiveness of our products. The combination of quality products and customer service has contributed to substantial sales growth.

Network Marketing has proven to be recession-resistant, as evidenced by its performance during the pandemic. Despite economic uncertainty and global lockdowns, this business model thrived by nurturing personal connections and offering lucrative income opportunities. It explored new avenues through word-of-mouth marketing, contributing to an increase in the country's GDP and per capita income. Remarkably, successful enterprises emerged even in times of economic instability.

The sales figures depicted in the data clearly demonstrate remarkable growth over the years. The high-quality products offered in this industry ensure customer satisfaction, further reinforcing its success.

The company really focuses on comprehensive training programs covering product knowledge, health-related information, and mental health and fitness awareness. In the network marketing industry, company training plays a pivotal role in driving success. These training initiatives are typically delivered through various methods, including seminars, workshops, mentoring, and conferences. Additionally, the company extends its offerings to include a wide range of Fast-Moving Consumer Goods (FMCG), providing training and services in this domain.

Furthermore, the company believes in the idea that you don't need a lot of heavy medicine to be healthy. Instead, it promotes the concept of happiness and well-being through minimal medication and maximal utilization of Ayurvedic products, known for their minimal side effects.

Ayurvedic products play a vital role in maintaining good health. These products are derived from natural sources such as herbs, plants, minerals, and other organic ingredients, formulated to support health & balance.

One key aspect of Ayurvedic products is the focus on prevention & maintaining the natural equilibrium of the body. They are tailored to individuals needs [vatta, pitta & kapha]. Known for their gentle & effective touch, they promote good health, improving digestion, reducing stress, & maintaining balanced energy levels. They serve as valuable complements to adapting to lifestyle changes and maintaining optimal health.

People have become more focused on developing their personalities. Network Marketing not only offers opportunities for financial growth but also serves as a platform for personal development & enhancement of their own personality. In Network Marketing, individuals learn the art of influencing others. It also encourages personal growth and self-motivation. It nurtures skills such as effective communication, relationships & self-confidence.

Today, individuals from various walks of life, including homemakers and those looking for ways to earn money without too much effort, are getting more interested in the direct-selling business model. And there are some really good reasons for that:

1. **Inclusivity:** Unlike many other businesses, direct selling doesn't discriminate based on age, qualifications, caste, colour, investment capacity, or prior experience. It offers an open and accessible entrepreneurial avenue to all.

2. **Diverse Product Range:** Direct selling companies often offer a wide range of high-quality products with attractive discounts, providing customers and sellers with appealing choices.

3. **Flexibility and Personal Growth:** This business model allows for unparalleled flexibility and personal growth. It offers opportunities for self-improvement, recognition, and passive income and requires a relatively low initial investment.

For homemakers, Network Marketing serves as a platform for personal growth and self-fulfilment. It helps them learn new things, feel accomplished, and boosts their confidence. It also lets them balance taking care of their homes with their dreams of having a business. Through effective personal development teachings and training, confidence levels are significantly boosted.

There is a quote written by **'Zig Ziglar' that states,**

"You don't build a business; you build people, and then people build the business."

Chapter 2

How to find the Right Company to start with

In today's world, many people want a better lifestyle, and that's why businesses like direct selling are becoming important. But to make this dream come true, you need to really focus on it because it's the key to reaching your big dreams.

However, it's essential to ensure that any chosen direct-selling company is operating within legal boundaries. Therefore, it's crucial to consider specific factors when evaluating the legitimacy of such companies.

1. Are You Getting a Product?

You have spent your money on a direct selling company, and they are not giving you the product you deserve. So, we need to keep a check on whether we are getting a deserved product in exchange for money or not.

Take a moment to assess whether the product you've purchased lives up to your expectations— a product that meets our needs, exceeds our expectations, and justifies our investment. Remember, your satisfaction matters.

Satisfactory product hona chahiye!

2. Check the Certification on their Website:

Look at the certificates on the company's website to make sure it's a real and trustworthy company. Reputable entities understand the significance of displaying their certifications openly to demonstrate compliance with legal requirements. By providing this information, businesses build trust and confidence among their customers. As consumers, we should always check for these certifications on a company's website to confirm their adherence to industry standards and regulations. So, before engaging with any entity, take a moment to verify their certifications, ensuring that you are dealing with a lawful and trustworthy organization.

Every entity needs to put their certifications on the website in order to be legal.

Certification check karne par legality ka pata chalega!

3. Legal Company will Always Deduct Your TDS & Deposit It to the Government:

A legitimate company will always deduct TDS (Tax Deducted at Source) from your payouts and promptly deposit it to the government. It's essential to verify if the TDS has been deducted from your earnings as per the prevailing tax regulations. You can easily check the status of your TDS payments on the income-tax website to ensure compliance. This practice not only ensures that you are fulfilling your tax obligations but also provides you with peace of mind, knowing that your taxes are being handled responsibly.

TDS kata toh legal hai!

4. Check for GST being Charged in Invoice:

Any legally authorized company will charge GST correctly without any falsity. Invoices issued by legitimate companies should always reflect the appropriate GST (Goods and Services Tax) charges, if applicable. It's essential for consumers to review their invoices to ensure that the correct GST amount has been included in the total cost. By having a proper breakdown of the GST on the invoice, customers can confidently verify the accuracy of the charges and confirm that the company is following the tax regulations diligently. Always check for GST on your invoices because it is a crucial aspect of responsible and lawful business practices.

GST dekho uska breakdown Dekho and validate.

5. Trademark Certificate/Product Approval Certificate:

After the product is launched, it is given to the consumer. If the consumer can see it, then it will be considered legal.

Getting a trademark certificate or product approval certificate is an important step after launching a product. When a consumer receives a product with these certificates, it assures them that the product is genuine, safe, and compliant with applicable regulations. Having these certificates gives confidence to the consumer, knowing that they are purchasing a real and authorized item.

Trademark dekho, Legal company pehchano

6. Company must have Submitted its Application to Government:

It's mandatory for any direct selling company to show the legalization & formulations to the government. As responsible consumers, we should always verify if a direct-selling company has fulfilled this essential requirement. Companies that have undergone the formalization process are more likely to be trustworthy and dependable partners. By doing this, we contribute to a safer and more reliable direct selling environment for everyone involved.

Documents Government ko dikhadie ya nahi?

In order to follow the guidelines & services for the same, Auretics registered itself for all the legal formalities, as they all have been entered on the website as well.

Consumer Benefit

Now that you have adhered to and know how to identify a reliable, legal and trustworthy company, it's essential to know what Consumer Benefit is.

Consumer benefit refers to the advantage or value that a consumer gets from using a product or service. It is the positive outcome or utility that a customer receives, addressing their needs, wants, or desires. It can take various forms, such as:

1. Functional Benefits:

These are the advantages that directly meet a customer's practical needs or solve a specific problem. For example, a smartphone's functional benefits may include a high-resolution camera, fast processing speed, and long battery life, which cater to users' communication and entertainment needs.

2. Emotional Benefits:

These are the intangible advantages that appeal to a customer's emotions and feelings. Emotional benefits can be associated with pleasure, joy, comfort, or a sense of belonging. For instance, a luxury watch may provide an emotional benefit of status and prestige to the wearer.

3. Cost-saving Benefits:

These benefits arise when a product or service helps consumers save money or get more value for their investment. For instance, energy-efficient appliances may offer cost-saving benefits by reducing electricity bills.

4. Convenience Benefits:

Convenience benefits simplify consumers' lives by providing ease of use, time-saving features, or accessibility. Online shopping platforms offer convenience benefits as they allow customers to shop from the comfort of their homes.

5. Health and Well-Being Benefits:

Products or services that contribute to improved health and well-being provide consumers with valuable benefits. This could include nutritious food products or fitness services that support a healthier lifestyle.

Consumer ko kya benefit hua?

There are certain consumer benefits, such as:

1. Retail Margin

2. Cashback

3. Accumulation

4. Return Policy

5. Buy 1 Get 1 on the range of products from Day 1

Chapter 3

Why become
a Digital Network Marketer

In today's era, there's a significant shift from traditional to digital living, revolutionizing the way people lead their lives, work, and engage with one another. The digital world brings many conveniences, letting us access information, services, and products easily, anytime and from anywhere. Here are some benefits of this shift:

- **Time Savings:**

  With digital options, there's no need to spend a lot of time commuting to an office. You can work or do tasks from wherever you are.

- **Cost Efficiency:**

  Digital ventures often require minimal overhead expenses, making it a cost-effective option.

- **Wider Reach:**

  Geographical distances don't matter as much. You can connect with people from different places, broadening your audience.

- **Work-from-Home (WFH):**

  This profession provides the opportunity to work from the comfort of one's Home, fostering independence and flexibility.

- **Flexible Timings:**

  The digital realm accommodates varying schedules, allowing individuals to work as per their availability.

- **Accessible Training:**

  Comprehensive training is readily available to guide newcomers, providing essential direction and insights.

Remember, aiming to become an online millionaire is an ambitious goal that requires commitment, strategic planning, and unwavering dedication.

Active vs Passive Income

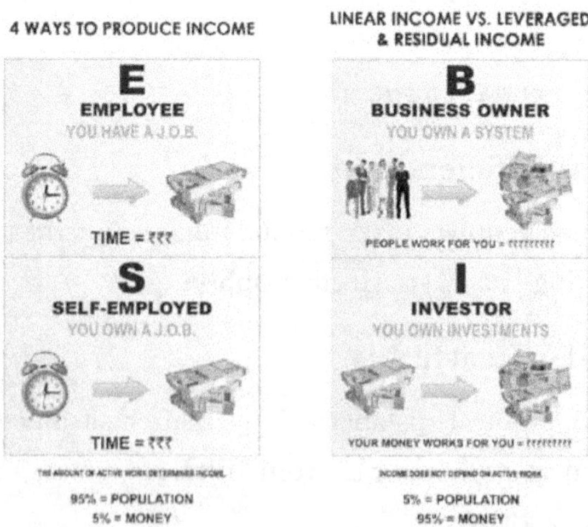

After careful research, the majority of people were divided into 4 categories abbreviated as ESBI. E stands for Employees, and S stands for Self-Employed, both forming part of Active Income. On the other hand, B stands for Big business owners, and I stands for Investors, both forming part of Passive Income.

(E) Employees sell their skills and their youth just to fulfil the dreams of their employer. The relationship between employees and employers can be complex and multifaceted, influenced by individual motivations, job satisfaction, work culture, and more.

(S) Self-employed also sell their skill and youth, but instead of selling it to someone else, they sell it to themselves.

For example: If a customer goes to a shop, the availability of the shopkeeper is a must to make the sale happen and earn money. If, due to any possible reason, the shopkeeper is unavailable at that moment, the sale will not take place, leading to no payment. Therefore, we can say that in the case of self-employed business owners, their availability and active involvement are crucial factors in attracting customers, making sales, and ultimately earning money.

(B) The whole money game changes at this point as the business owner creates a system and earns a huge amount of money. They purchase the skills and time of their employees so that they can earn well and fulfil their dreams. Whether they go to the office or not, their business will operate independently and keep on generating money for them.

(I) Investors are the ones who have strong business and political connections, and they own investments in the share market or real estate and earn a hefty profit from their investments. Investors play a critical role by deploying their capital in various asset classes to generate returns and build wealth.

Only 5% of the persons are Investors and Business Owners; the rest fall into the category of Employees and Self-employed. The irony is that 95% of people (employees and self-employed) have 5% of the money, and 5% of people (business owners and investors) have 9% of the money.

So, if we need to change our lifestyle, we must get ourselves into the right box and shift our income from an active to a passive source. The real issue is,

How can you make this shift?

If you need to be on the right side (B and I), you must have:

1. Crores of rupees

2. Good skills

3. A big heart to pay lacs of rent for your area

4. Man-management capabilities

5. Risk-taking capabilities

Most individuals cannot leave their current profession and risk their lifetime savings to start a business. For this very reason, we have created Auretics Business, which doesn't require high investment or any risk. Moreover, we train people about Auretics

Business with the best trainers in the industry for FREE and help them develop their skills and inculcate man-management capabilities.

By becoming an employee, you will keep working harder and harder to build someone else's empire while you get pennies.

Let me give you another example.

Year	Work (8 hours daily)	Income (₹)
35 year		
	12000 hours	1,05,06,262 (10% increment per year)
30 year		
	12000 hours	74,90,820 (10% increment per year)
25 year		
	12000 hours	53,40,851 (10% increment per year)
20 year		
	12000 hours	38,07,953 (10% increment per year)
15 year		
	12000 hours	27,15,018 (10% increment per year)
10 year		
	12000 hours	19,35,770 (10% increment per year)
5 year		
	12000 hours	13,80,177 (10% increment per year)
1 year		
	2400 hours	2,40,000
0 year		
Total Working Hours (35 years) 84,000 hours		**Total Income ₹6,50,45,848**

Imagine starting your career with an annual salary of Rs. 2,40,000, with a modest 7% annual increment. By the time you retire, your income will have grown to an impressive Rs. 23 lakh per year, resulting in a lifetime income of Rs. 3.31 crore. However, it's worth noting that even after working diligently for 30 years, the income potential in your last 5 years just before retirement will be Rs. 1.05 crore for that period.

As an employee, your hard work may not always translate into proportional financial rewards. Incremental raises often struggle to keep up with the rising cost of everyday expenses. What's more, retirement typically means a complete halt in salaried income.

Self-employment offers the opportunity to earn in line with your time and skills invested. However, it may limit your personal and family time. As you age, your ability to invest time in your profession may also decrease, impacting your income.

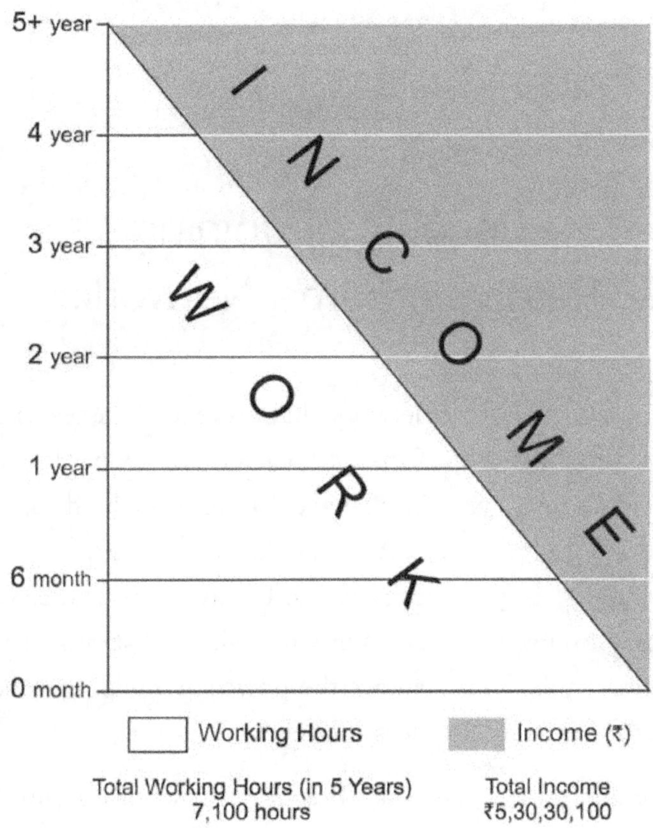

5+ year
4 year
3 year
2 year
1 year
6 month
0 month
INCOME
WORK
Working Hours
Income (₹)
Total Working Hours (in 5 Years)
7,100 hours
Total Income
₹5,30,30,100

Chapter 4

Benefits of Joining Passive Income Networks

Join passive income networks like Auretics Business. Initially, you may invest more effort for relatively lower income, but as your team grows, you won't have to work as hard, and your income will go up a lot. In Auretics Business, your income grows exponentially as your team expands, and you gradually find yourself working less while still witnessing substantial earnings. This remarkable feature shows the power of building leadership within the Auretics Business model.

A quick look at Auretics Business shows it's a simple but really rewarding opportunity. The Super Infinity Compensation Plan ensures substantial earnings, while lifestyle rewards, including luxury cars, vacations, and funds for home purchases or renovations, add an enticing dimension to the experience.

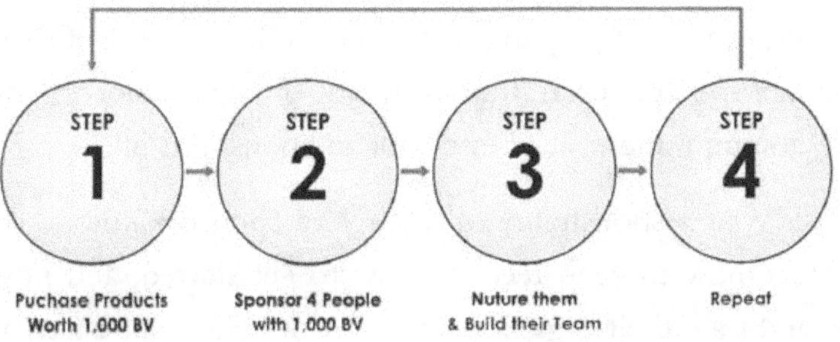

We have created a simple 4-step formula for you to follow:

1. Start by using Auretics' products yourself. Purchase and use the daily-use products.

2. Sponsor 4 people under you and make them a user of Auretics products.

3. Share your experiences with them and help them in making their own teams.

4. Repeat these steps.

Therefore, direct selling involves sharing the product you like and getting paid for it. It further involves building an organisation for yourself and your sponsors, where many distributors join and start consumption or retail.

It's not about going door-to-door every day or calling on strangers. Rather, it is about sponsoring and teaching your team.

Sponsoring and teaching play a very vital role in direct selling; it's like sponsoring someone and then teaching them how to do what you are doing, i.e., building a business of their own. I emphasize that there is a big difference between sponsoring someone and just signing them up. When you SPONSOR someone, you are committing to them. If you are not willing to make a commitment, it's better not to sponsor at all.

It is your responsibility to teach your sponsors how to order products, how to keep records, how to get started, and how to build and train their organisation. Sponsoring is what makes your business grow.

As your organisation grows, you are working towards becoming an INDEPENDENT, SUCCESSFUL person. You are becoming your own BOSS.

So, remember, here, a person won't make money just by selling the products; they make money by building an organisation. So, this is the sole purpose of this book: to teach you the things you need to know to build an organisation.

Direct Selling is a method of making sales in which we do not sponsor people in Direct Selling; rather, we sponsor them in the Direct Selling System. The point is we don't have to tell them how to sell. Rather, we must teach them how to TEACH and SPONSOR and build a large, successful team. And we can do this WITHOUT SELLING ANYTHING, just by TEACHING & SPONSORING.

To get sponsorship, make sure to emphasize to your team that staying in regular contact with people at least three levels below them is the secret to successful duplication and expansion.

When it comes to sponsoring, it's crucial to stress the importance of true duplication. Encourage your team members to convey to their contacts that in order to replicate their success, they should aim to build strong connections at least three levels deep. By doing so, they can ensure that their efforts multiply and create a strong foundation for growth within the organisation. In this way, each member's success will inspire and empower others, leading to a robust and thriving team.

Example: Let's say you are here (Draw a circle and put YOU in the middle). You sponsor Sajal (Draw another circle under the one with YOU in it. Write Sajal in it and connect circles with a line). Now, if you leave and Sajal doesn't know what to do (because you haven't taught her), then that's the end of it. But if you teach Sajal how to sponsor, and she sponsors Radhika, you are ONLY beginning to DUPLICATE Yourself.

But, if Sajal doesn't learn how to teach Radhika to sponsor, then it will fizzle out, and that's the end of it. You have to teach Sajal how to guide Radhika in sponsoring. Then, she can sponsor Ram further, and the cycle goes on. So, I emphasize you have to go THREE LEVEL DEEP! You have nothing until you are three levels deep, and only then YOU ARE DUPLICATED.

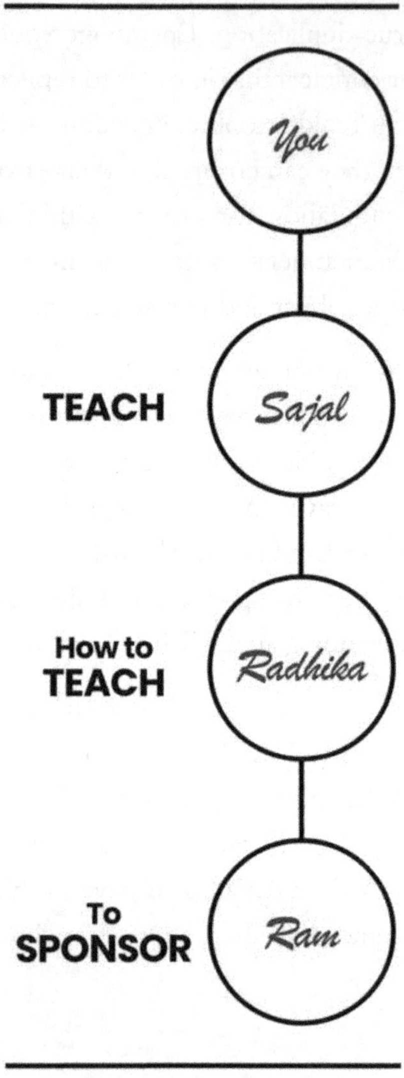

Paisa kamana hai toh teen levels tak padhao!

Do you love to travel? If yes, then you will love my next example.

Let's imagine you want to take a trip in the family car, leave rainy Delhi, and drive to sunny Jaipur. The sunshine represents reaching the top of the program that you are in. When you get there, you are successful; you're at the TOP (Jaipur).

The **FIRST THING** you have to do is GET IN and GET STARTED. So, nobody in DIRECT SELLING has made a lot of money unless they first got started.

The **SECOND THING** you need to do is buy PETROL. As you travel to the top (Jaipur), you will use up fuel (Products), and it will be necessary to replace them. So, direct selling works best with consumable products.

The **THIRD THING** is to get into High Gear. We all know that nobody starts in High Gear. We all start in Neutral. So, to get your car in gear, you must sponsor someone into the business. When you sponsor someone, you are in FIRST Gear. I believe you should be in four gear four times with 4 serious people. Also, teach them how to get into first gear by sponsoring someone.

...and Buy
More products

The **FOURTH THING** is to use the time to SHARE your products with the people who are going with you. Again, we say you don't have to SELL the products; you need to SHARE the products.

You are required to do four things:

1. Get in- Get started & Use the Products.

2. Shift into high gear (Share with friends).

3. Make their team.

4. Repeat.

Here, note that if you don't do number 3 (sponsoring and getting into high gear) and do more of number 4, you will never get out of the driveway. Once you grasp this concept, start developing a proper direct-selling attitude.

So, STOP looking for people who want to sell. START looking for people who want to earn an extra income without having to go to work. The answer is EVERYBODY. Everybody would like to have that kind of dough coming. Give 5 to 10 hours of your time each week to learning. When you learn and understand, then only you can teach the presentations to others. The book you are reading right now is the key to the success of tomorrow. Remember, to get into direct selling, you must have a SPONSOR. If your sponsor is a real "sponsor", he will help you with the first 5 people. So, it's a HELPING RELATIONSHIP.

DIGGING DOWN TO BEDROCK

Many times, when you sponsor someone, they may feel discouraged to start something new.

Motivation is the fuel that drives success in network marketing. It is the enthusiasm and determination that keeps individuals focused on their goals and propels them to move forward, even when things get tough. In this dynamic industry, where building strong relationships and expanding one's network is paramount, motivation becomes a crucial factor. It empowers marketers to consistently reach out to new prospects, share their products or services passionately, and inspire others to join their teams. By harnessing the power of motivation, we can unlock unprecedented levels of success in the world of network marketing.

Imagine your journey to success as the construction of a towering office building. At the outset, when you start by sponsoring your first five dedicated individuals, it's like breaking ground with a simple shovel and spade.

As you progress to the second level, teaching your team to sponsor 25 people, you'll need more powerful tools, like bulldozers, to dig deeper into your goals. The true foundation of your success is forming.

When you've imparted your knowledge to a group that sponsors 125 people, you've reached bedrock. Now, you can begin your ascent. At this point, your progress becomes visible, much like a building that starts to rise.

Don't be discouraged if you don't see immediate results. Remember, a strong foundation takes time to build. You can only expect visible results when you've gone down at least four levels, indicating that you're now constructing floors and becoming visible on your path to success.

*"Sponsor and teach at least 4-level down,
and you will see Success."*

~Karishma Gupta

How can you identify a Gold Ship?

DIRECT SELLING gives people an opportunity to chase their dreams. So, here, just imagine, there are three types of ships in the sea. Label the first ship as "GOLD", the second as "SILVER", and the third ship as "M.T." (Empty).

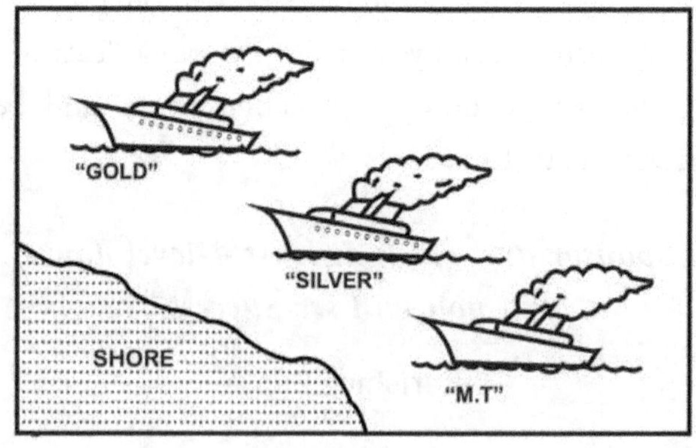

These ships represent people in the organization.

Here, the Gold ships are the ones who have sponsored and left on their own, thinking they don't need any help or direction.

M.T. ships are the ones that have been in the program, and you still have to convince them every time you see them. When you sponsor someone into the business, they come as a Silver ship. So, it's determined by how you work with them and whether they turn into Gold or M.T.

So, how can you identify a **Gold Ship** or **Serious Person** for your business?

1. **Eager to Learn:** They will call you anytime for all the answers they need.

2. **Ask for Help:** They want training and teachings for regular sponsoring.

3. **Excited about the Business:** They understand enough about the program and also are excited to know how the program works.

4. **Make Commitments:** They are buying and using the products and spending their time learning.

5. **Goal-oriented:** Goals help drive a person to get what they want.

6. **Positive Attitude:** They always have a positive approach towards each and everything.

7. **They are fun to be with:** They look forward to visiting close friends and relatives.

8. **Passionate Workers:** Passion-oriented workers who work with a drive in them.

So, if you really want to know who the Gold Ship is? Please look out for the qualities discussed above. I want you to be aware of three basic words:

1. **Expose**

2. **Involve**

3. **Upgrade**

The first thing you have to do is to EXPOSE the person in the business you are in. Once you have exposed them, get them INVOLVED. Once they are involved, they will be thinking about how far they can go, and then they will be UPGRADED constantly.

So, expose them to Direct Selling by explaining various methods (Retail Sales, Traditional Sales, Direct Sales, Direct Selling).

Also, people need to understand that WHEN YOU CALL, they realize you are not PUSHING them; rather, you WANT TO HELP THEM SOLVE THEIR PROBLEM.

"Don't Push To Sell; Push To Help And Teach."

~Karishma Gupta

So, when you call an Empty Ship, you get the feeling that they are not thrilled about you calling them. This is a very good indication that they feel you are being pushy and bugging them. They think that you are pressuring them. They are the ones you have to prove again and again.

On the other hand, if you call a Gold Ship, they simply understand that you are calling them because you want to help them. This can easily be traced through their conversational tone.

Here's a tip: Never call your downline and ask how much they sold last week. Because if you do, they might feel offended to go to the market and SELL directly. Rather, our motto is to share, sponsor, and build an organization.

So, money will come automatically if you help people to succeed.

Remember Zig Zaglor's advice: You will have anything in this world that you want simply by helping other people enough to get what they want.

So!! GOLD SHIP KIS KISKO BANNNA HAI???

In the world of prospecting, we often refer to it as the "third-party invitation." But what exactly does this term mean?

Let me illustrate with an example: Imagine you know someone named "xyz." Instead of approaching "xyz" directly and asking if they want to earn extra income, you take a different approach. You go to someone like Carol and say, "I've recently started an exciting new business, and I could use your help. Do you happen to know anyone who might be interested in earning some extra income?" Notice how you're asking for a referral to a THIRD PARTY. If Carol knows someone, she'll likely respond positively, as many people are interested in additional income opportunities.

If you try this approach with multiple people, you'll likely receive similar responses. They'll ask, "What is it?" because they might be intrigued by the idea of earning extra income themselves.

Your response should then be, "Have you heard about DIRECT SELLING?" If they answer "Yes," you can delve into what they know about it. Often, people have concerns or fears about starting such a business, like the fear of rejection. Nobody enjoys being rejected, so the key is to engage with more people to reduce the chances of facing rejection.

Think of this process as launching various ships. Some of these ships will turn into gold carriers, as discussed earlier. However, there are only two possible outcomes when you launch a ship: it will either float or sink. If it sinks, you find yourself on the dock. But if it floats, you have the opportunity to transform it into a vessel that carries gold – a valuable and fruitful connection. So, don't be discouraged by the occasional "sinks" – keep launching those ships and seeking the ones that will carry you to success.

Gold Ship Ban Jao Or Laabh Uthao

Now, imagine becoming a gold ship is like creating a fire. Think of having lots of logs from a tree to fuel that fire. This example helps us understand the process better.

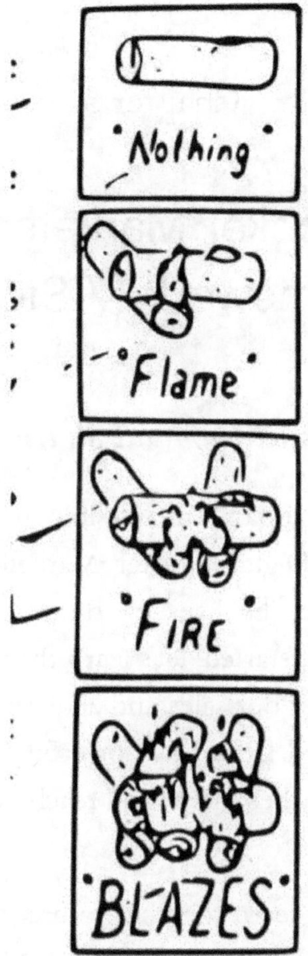

If you have one log, you have nothing. With two, you will have a flame. If you put three logs together, you will have a fire.

Put all of them together, and you will have a BLAZE.

So, GET ON A BLAZE, get them Sizzlingggg, get on FIRE!!!!!!!!!

Chapter 5

Rocket Marketeer Framework (7 Steps)

Ab 7 Steps Ki Kahaani Shuru Hoti Hai

Becoming a millionaire is possible with a simple 7-step formula called the Digital Rocket Marketer framework. This formula has changed the lives of thousands and millions of people. Before we get started, let's learn the four important steps that will help us boost our sales and achieve great success. Many have already benefited from this powerful framework, and now it's our turn to follow these steps and reach new heights in Digital Network Marketing.

Let's explore and learn together to unlock our true potential and achieve amazing things in the business world. The opportunity is right here, and we can start this journey today! In this figure, there are two types of problems:

1st problem – No or few customers.

2nd problem – Overburdened with customers [customer overflowing more than the capacity].

If we want our problem to be the 2nd one, then we need to follow a Four-Phase selling way in which the whole world is currently working.

We receive numerous complaints as people's minds have stopped working due to being badly overburdened with all the happenings around. In this figure, you can see the traditional way of selling where people are overburdened, and their minds have stopped working. On the other hand, we can see the 4 –phase selling way, which needs to be injected into the brains of people. So, a few things need to be remembered before we follow the 7- steps of the Digital Network (N/W) Marketer Framework.

1. Do not showcase your company or product on the first go. Do not tell the company name or product's name to anyone.

2. Avoid displaying your company's name in your profile. While it may make some people happy, it's a big NO. Never showcase your company name in your profile.

    We need to make sure that our bio, cover picture, profile picture, etc., are up-to-date. Present yourself with a tag like Health Coach, Immunity Expert, Stress Receiver, Fitness Advisor, etc.

    Also, you need to share those types of posts and managers which are related to certain kinds of topics, such as:

    i. Good health (Physical + Mental)

    ii. Fitness (Gym, Yoga & Exercise)

    iii. Meditation

 iv. Food

 v. Travel

 vi. Products/services that you like.

Need to stop certain things like Commenting, Sharing & Posting:

 i. Politics

 ii. Religion

 iii. Caste

 iv. Body type (fat/Slim/Black/White/Tall/Short) of someone

 v. Gender discrimination

 vi. Advertisements or inappropriate content

Let's Begin The Journey of 7 Steps

Step 1: Prepare Your Niche

We need to understand the needs of the customer, what they actually want, and need to prepare Niche accordingly. We need to choose a single product, and aim to be the KING of that product.

Understanding the needs of your customers is crucial because it entails:

1. **Targeted Marketing:** It involves focusing your marketing efforts on a specific audience or segment of the market.

2. **Customer Satisfaction:** Meeting and exceeding customer expectations leads to positive word-of-mouth, repeat business, and sustainable growth.

3. **Competitive Advantage:** A competitive advantage gives a business a unique edge over its rivals, allowing it to outperform and stand out in the marketplace.

4. **Improved Customer Engagement:** Improved customer engagement strengthens the bond between a business and its customers, leading to increased trust and loyalty.

We also need to understand ourselves while preparing for our Niche. Before understanding the customer, it is important to understand yourself:

i. You CANNOT become an expert in every field.

ii. You CANNOT become an expert in every product.

iii. You CANNOT cater to the demands of every market.

iv. You CANNOT become a specialist in everything.

To become the king in your chosen domain, your product must possess certain key qualities:

– **Intrinsic Interest:** First and foremost, the product you focus on should genuinely interest you. It should ignite your passion and keep you engaged in the long run. An authentic interest is your foundation for success.

– **Inherent Value:** The product you choose to master should offer real value to your target audience. It should address their needs or desires, solving problems or fulfilling aspirations. True kings create value for others.

- **Uniqueness and Uniqueness:** Your product should stand out from the crowd. It must possess qualities that make it one-of-a-kind and impossible for others to duplicate. Being unique gives you a competitive edge.

- **Scarcity:** To truly reign supreme, your chosen product should be scarce or at least appear that way. It should be something exclusive, available only through your expertise or effort. Scarcity adds allure and exclusivity to your domain.

Therefore, focus only on a SINGLE product that possesses the following qualities:

1. **Your Interest:** Pick only 1 product (preferably the best-selling product of your company) that genuinely interests you.

2. **Value:** Ensure that the product offers significant value to the customer.

3. **Rare:** Make sure the product is exclusively available through you.

4. **Inimitable:** Choose a product that cannot be easily copied, such as through self-research or a patented product.

For Example:

Ram, who is diabetic, is fed up with the side effects of allopathic medicines.

He is also confused because of so many online choices and is not able to decide the right herbal solution for his needs.

Now, Ram wants some help in making an intelligent buying solution.

Your role is to provide the right solution to Ram and help him by offering accurate decisions.

When You will Understand him, He will Follow You, Understand You, and will buy from You.

Remember, when making any post, share it on a relevant online platform or send it to a relevant person. Don't send all the posts to everyone in one go. Make selections and send them reminders at regular intervals.

We can provide MCB (Mass control bait - Any Title by which you can conquer masses) to the people as, considering the high ratio of diabetic individuals:

> ***"Control your sugar without taking any extra tablets, even when you don't want to exercise."***

Step 2: Gain Traffic

In this section, we will understand the Traffic Sources and identify which Traffic actually works. Gain traffic means "utilizing social media platforms and optimizing your online presence for search engines."

Following are the sources of Contacts that we can have:

1. **Contacts that you OWN include:**

     i. Friends

     ii. Relatives

     iii. Office Colleagues

     iv. People in your Society

     v. Family WhatsApp/Telegram Contacts

2. **Contacts that you BUY include:**

     i. Pay-per-click ads

     ii. SEO on Website

     iii. Social Media Ads (Facebook/Instagram/YouTube)

3. **Contacts that you EARN include:**

     i. Referrals

     ii. Joint Ventures

     iii. Partnership

     iv. Networking at an event

     v. Common Social Groups

4. **Contacts that are STRANGER include:**

     i. E-Mail Database

     ii. SMS/WhatsApp Database

There are certain traffics that are easiest to start with and vary in terms of cost, effectiveness, and efficiency:

- **Easiest to Start:** Contacts that you OWN

- **Most Expensive:** Contacts that you BUY

- **Most Effective:** Contacts that you EARN

- **Least Effective:** Contacts that are STRANGERS

So, let's start with contacts that you OWN

Social Media:

1. Find a good 20 profiles (that you don't know).

2. Send them a message.

3. Ask them about their Profession.

4. Follow up with messages every alternate day.

Example:

Dear <NAME>,

Maine aapki profile dekhi, main aapki profile se bohot prabhavit hua.

Main aapke profession ke baare mei aur janna chahata hoon.

Waiting for your reply.

Aapka Friend,

Arjun Gupta

Diabetic Expert

8282828728

Thank you very much <NAME>. You are in a very good profession. I am helping <Teacher/Homemakers/Accountants/Students> to grow their own business without Investment. My phone number is 8282828728. Can I have your number?

Contacts That You BUY

1. **Pay-per-click ads:**

    Imagine you want people to know about your online store. You pay a little bit of money every time someone clicks on an ad that shows up when they search for things like "cool clothes online." These clicks lead to people visiting your store, and those visitors are contacts you essentially "bought."

2. **SEO on Website:**

    Let's say you have a blog about video games. By making your blog easily findable on Google, people who are interested in video games might discover your site. Even though you didn't directly buy these visitors, the effort you put into making your site visible can be seen as a way of getting contacts.

3. **Social Media Ads (Facebook/Instagram):**

    Picture this: You love baking and want to sell your homemade cookies. You decide to use Facebook and Instagram to show your cookies to people who might be interested. You spend some money to make sure your posts reach more people. When these people like or comment on your posts, they become contacts you reached by spending money on social media ads.

Contacts That You EARN

WhatsApp:

1. Send a request message to all of your contacts.

2. Join maximum groups today.

3. Design your introduction message.

4. Put it in your DP & Status.

Example:

Dear <NAME>,

Main pichhle kuchh samay se <DIABETES YA JO BHI AAPKA PRODUCT HAI> kaise control ki jaaye iss topic par research kar raha tha. Iss topic par main kuch important jaankari logon tak pahunchana chahta hun. Apse ek request hai ki aap jitne bhi groups main add hain kripya mujhe unn groups main add kijiye taaki main <DIABETES> topic par logon ki madad kar sakun.

Reply zarur kijiyega ki aapne kitnw group me join karwaya hai.

Thanks,

Arjun Gupta

Diabetes Expert

8282828728

Facebook Groups

- Please prepare a comment bank.

- Utilize the Notes App.

- Write your and someone else's good comments in that bank.

- YouTube Videos/Shorts.

- Instagram Reels/IGTV.

- Facebook Videos/Stories.

These remarkable video-sharing platforms have one thing in common: lots of people who really like them. They are beloved by people, and this popularity makes them an invaluable tool for personal brand building.

In the world of personal branding, these platforms offer an exceptional opportunity to showcase your talents, expertise, and personality to a vast and appreciative audience. Whether you're an aspiring influencer, a content creator, or an expert in your field, utilizing the power of these platforms can help you establish and enhance your personal brand excitingly and dynamically.

Facebook Groups

1. Open your Facebook account.

2. Go to Groups.

3. Search for the relevant groups as per your product.

4. Start joining these groups.

5. Remember, do not join more than 5 groups in a day. **(Else Facebook will Ban You).**

Contacts That You Earn (Facebook Group)	
There are 2 types of groups:	
1.	**Public Groups:** Public Groups are those you can join without the approval of the Admin. However, in most Public Groups, you may not have permission to post.
2.	**Private Groups:** Private Group is the group where you can join only after admin approval. In Most Private Group you may not have permission to post.

Post Permissions

Prospecting with Permission to Post:

1. Share information about a relevant issue and provide a link for a webinar or online video.

2. Avoid directly posting about the product; focus on presenting a solution without sounding salesy or spammy.

3. Limit your posts to once a week to avoid being identified as spam and banned by the group admin.

Inspecting without Permission to Post:

1. In groups where posting isn't allowed, introduce yourself in the comment section.

2. Avoid posting about your product or unrelated content.

3. Do not post too many comments on the same groups. (Max 3-5).

4. To stand out from the crowd, write a medium-length comment of 4-5 lines.

5. Posting relevant details is very easy; you may message like this to gain attention:

Dear <NAME>,

You have rightly mentioned that "Diabetes is a household problem" in your recent post. Taking care of our health collectively is crucial.

Your post has the potential to change many lives. Please keep sharing these kinds of posts, and I will wait for your next post.

Thank you very much.

Your friend,

Arjun Gupta

Diabetes expert

8282828728/support@auretics.com

Contacts That Are Strangers

- **Email Database:**

  Think of it like getting a list of email addresses from a company you don't know. These are people who have never heard about you or your business. Sending them emails is like introducing yourself to strangers online.

- **SMS:**

  Imagine having a list of phone numbers from a source you're not familiar with. These are individuals who haven't given you their numbers directly. Sending them messages is like texting or messaging strangers on your phone.

Step 3: Marketing Message

(What and how to say that will trigger people to come and Join You)

In this figure, you can see:

EXAMPLE 1

Problem 1: I will teach you the concept of Physics.

Problem 2: I will teach you how to get 90% in Physics.

Which solution to the problem is better for you?

The second solution, stating, "I will teach you how to get 90% in Physics", sounds more believable and authentic than the first one.

It represents the basic title that is called MCB (Mass Control Bait) here to the customers so they represent the business well.

EXAMPLE 2

Marketing Message

Here, you can easily see the Title of the Book "Naura -Hayde: Astrological Love." This was the cover page of the book where the author was unable to sell copies of the book and was very disheartened.

In the second image, you can see the cover page of the book where the title of the book has been changed to: 'How to Satisfy A Woman Every Time and Have Her Beg for More' by Naura Hayden.

It turned out to be a BIG BLAST sale. Just by changing the MCB (Mass control Bait) Title, several copies were sold. This effectively shows how Marketing your message plays a significant role in the productivity of your Sales.

Which will work better

Referring to this figure, no one will do business or any type of dealings with this kind of person. Everyone prefers someone who is confident enough to make proper deals and look happy and satisfied.

Which will work better

So, this looks better if compared with Mass control bait (MCB) as *'Kya aap apni team ke Amitabh Bachchan banna chahte hain? (Janiye vo 7 raaz jo aapko apne* business *ka* superstar *banate hain.)''*

Step 4: Invitation for an online Meeting/Webinar

(Webinars are the best attention Grabbers)

In the webinar, we need to inject some major valuables to the consumers: **Don't Sell the PRODUCT, Sell the SOLUTION.**

Invitation for an online meeting/webinar:

A webinar must follow this sequence:

1. **Opening:**

   Authority Building.

2. **Transformative Content:**

   Share something the customer is unaware of that can change their perception through powerful content.

3. **Bridge:**

   Recap everything and provide them with 2 options.

4. **Closing:**

   Give them a Call to Action.

If you need to find the best topic for the webinar, follow these major steps:

1. Open the browser in Incognito Mode.

2. Go to Answer ThePublic.com.

3. Search your product's niche (Eg: "Diabetes").

You will get the most/frequently asked questions that you can answer.

Creating compelling content for a webinar is a crucial task. Here are steps to guide you in crafting the best content:

- Start by searching for ChatGPT, a valuable resource for content creation.

- Specify the topic you're focused on for your webinar.

- Adapt the topic as needed to align with your objectives.

- Engage in a conversation with ChatGPT to generate more content ideas and insights.

- Feel free to ask for details in your preferred language.

These steps will help you utilize AI to its optimum, especially ChatGPT, to curate content that resonates with your audience and makes your webinar a success.

Step 5: Sending Leads To Your Product's Landing Page

Once the webinar has been successfully conducted, follow up with your potential customers regarding any question they may have in their mind.

Next, send a link to your customers for the landing page of the product, where they can see a recap of your webinar and get more details about the product.

Finally, you must follow up with a strong Call to Action (CTA) encouraging them to buy the product and add it to their basket for checkout.

Selling is Service

The Art of Sales and Follow-Ups

In this section, we delve into the intricate world of salesmanship and the critical role that follow-ups play in securing lasting customer relationships.

The Temptation of Marketing

The stark contrast between reality and marketing is a powerful driver of customer appeal. One picture shows the plain truth, and the other reveals the attractive version advertisers want you to see. To grab people's attention, it's important to understand and acknowledge this difference.

Step 6: Making the Sale - The Final Follow-Up

Selling isn't just a transaction; it's a service. To close the deal, consider these essential steps:

Objection Handling: Address any concerns or doubts potential customers may have.

- Providing Offers: Present enticing offers that make the decision to buy irresistible.

- Money-Back Guarantee: Reassure customers of their satisfaction with a money-back guarantee.

- Product Guidance: Educate customers on how to effectively use your product.

By doing these steps, you make the final sale, which is a really important part of the customer's journey.

Step 7: Follow-Ups for Re-Order

The post-sale follow-up is more critical than its pre-sale counterpart for several reasons:

- **Customer Assurance:** Customers need to know you're there to support them even after the sale.

- **Product Usage Reminder:** Encourage customers to use your product for desired results and future purchases.

- **Offering More:** Once customers have experienced your products, introduce them to additional options within your product range.

This part explains how to sell things well and keep customers happy by staying in touch after they buy. It helps your business do well for a long time.

Follow-ups after Closing a Sale is essential for:

1. Customer Satisfaction

2. Re-order

3. Cross-Sell

4. Upsell/Down sell

Timely follow-up is the key to retaining customers and solving their problems. You must follow up with your customer, lost customer, or prospect within 24 hours to retain them and leave them satisfied with your product/services.

Chapter 6

How to make these Steps EASY

A customer appreciates good service. Always be available for the customers and resolve their issues timely.

You must establish your value or design your own Unique Selling Proposition (USP).

Creating Your Unique Value

In this section, we explore the essential elements to craft your distinctive value proposition.

Building Your Value: A Five-Step Guide

To establish your unique value, consider these five crucial steps:

- **Goal Achievement:** Your journey begins by helping others attain their aspirations. Be the bridge that leads them to success.

- **Understanding the Problem:** Dive deep into the root causes of the challenges your audience faces. Knowing the background is key to providing effective solutions.

- **Dream Fulfillment:** Inspire and assist in realizing their dreams. Show them that their aspirations are not just within reach but entirely attainable.

- **Sharing Business Secrets:** Build trust by sharing insider knowledge. Solve their problems and make things smooth.

- **Easy & Authentic Pathways:** Guide them along straightforward and trustworthy paths to reach their goals. Share ideas, and tools, and engage in supportive activities that make their journey smoother.

Calculating the Costs

Creating this value requires an investment of resources:

- **Cost:** Financial resources to support your efforts.

- **Time:** Dedication to research, planning, and execution.

- **Efforts:** Your commitment and hard work.

Understanding the costs involved is essential in crafting your unique value proposition.

The cost required to perform all 7 steps are:

Particulars	Cost	Product
Understanding the Needs of a Customer	-	-
Gain Traffic	9999	Online NM Course
Marketing Message	3999	Canva (Yearly)
Inviting for an Online Meeting/Webinar	10200	Webinar Kit (Yearly)
Sending Leads to Product's Landing Page	11500	Figma (Yearly)
Making the Sale	17988	Shopify (Yearly)
Follow-ups for Re-order	14400	Galla box (Yearly)
Total	**68,086**	

The time required to perform all 7 Steps are:

Particulars	Time
Understanding the Needs of a Customer	6 Months
Gain Traffic	2 Months (Online Course)
Marketing Message	15 Days
Inviting for an Online Meeting/Webinar	20 Days
Sending Leads to Product's Landing Page	1 Month
Making the Sale	18 Months
Follow-ups for Re-order	15 Days
Total	**12 Months**

Always invest in learning. By investing in learning and development, direct sellers can enhance their skills, refine their strategies, and unlock new opportunities for success in the ever-evolving world of direct selling.

6 Month Estimate with Auretics Limited

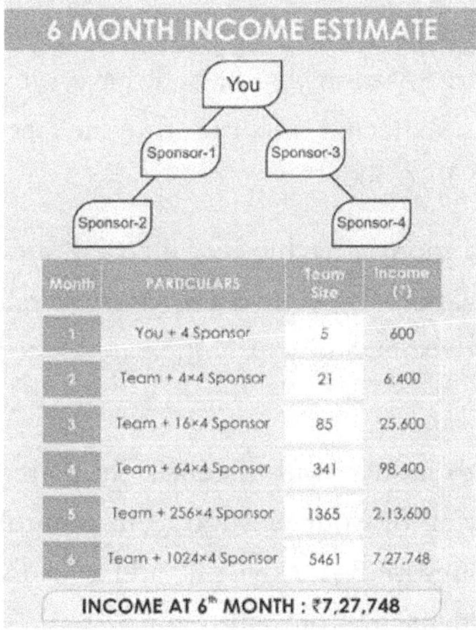

Month	PARTICULARS	Team Size	Income (₹)
1	You + 4 Sponsor	5	600
2	Team + 4×4 Sponsor	21	6,400
3	Team + 16×4 Sponsor	85	25,600
4	Team + 64×4 Sponsor	341	98,400
5	Team + 256×4 Sponsor	1365	2,13,600
6	Team + 1024×4 Sponsor	5461	7,27,748

With Auretics you only have to sponsor 2 individuals in both organisations who are interested in creating a passive income source as Auretics Advisors in a month. Then teach them how to get started with their choice of products. Finally, they need to sponsor 2 individuals in both of their organisations and repeat the process.

Initially you might find that the income you are getting is very less, but gradually, month-on-month, you will notice an exponential increase in your income.

Let me explain you how:

In the first month when you join and sponsor 2-2 individuals in both of your organisations, your total team strength will be 5 Advisors, and your estimated income in the first month will be Rs.600.

In your second month, they will sponsor two advisors for each of their organisations, and you'll have a total team of 21 Advisors. Your expected income for the second month is estimated to be Rs.6,400.

By the third month, having recruited 2-2 individuals in both of your organizations by your team, your overall team strength will reach 85 Advisors, and your anticipated income is estimated to be Rs.25,600.

In the fourth month, with a consistent pattern of recruiting 2 individuals by all of your existing team monthly, your team is projected to comprise 341 Advisors, and your expected income remains at Rs.98,400.

The same pattern will create a team size of 1,365 in the fifth month, and your income will reach Rs.2,13,600.

By the end of the sixth month, with a steady recruitment of 2 individuals by your team on both organisations, combined with regular training, your team is projected to reach a strength of 5,461 Advisors, and the expected income is estimated at Rs.7,27,748.

Amazing, isn't it… That's the power of Compounding.

Now, a question may arise in your mind: will this only happen only when everything is going well, and are these just theoretical aspects?

We would like to remind you that although recruiting 2 individuals with a zeal to do something in a month is not that difficult, let's say you have not achieved 100%, but only 80%, even then, your monthly payout will be Rs.5,82,198.

In case you are able to do only 50%, still your monthly payout will be Rs.3,63,874.

Not only that, even if you are able to reach 20%, then also your payout will be Rs.1,45,549 per month.

Even if you are not able to achieve 20%, but only 10% achievement will give you a payout of Rs.72,774 per month.

In the end, due to your daily efforts, even if you are able to achieve only 10%, then also you don't have to get disheartened, as a simple 5% achievement will also give you a passive income of Rs.36,874 per month.

Now, that is amazing…

When you choose Auretics as your career, your income grows exponentially every month.

Choose Your Path

We explore two distinct options for your journey to success.

1. **Option A: On your own**

    i. **Endless Search for Customers:** Keep looking for new customers all the time.

    ii. Round-the-Clock Effort: Work constantly to maintain your sales and income.

    iii. Constant Team Follow-Ups: Keep pushing your team to make purchases.

2. **Option B: Have us by your side.**

    i. Great Lifestyle: Enjoy the rewards of an incredible lifestyle, a life you've always dreamt of.

    ii. Motivate and Inspire Your Team: Lead by example and earn the respect and admiration of your team members.

    iii. Work from Home: Enjoy the freedom of working from the comfort of your home.

    iv. Residual Income: Secure your future with income that keeps flowing in.

    v. National Reach: Cast your net wide and find leads all across the country.

    vi. Elevate Others: Help others transform their lives for the better.

Chapter 7

How to fulfil all your Dreams

AURETICS LIMITED: Your Gateway to Success

At AURETICS LIMITED, we offer you more than just a business opportunity:

- **Guidance from Experts:** Benefit from our Hand-Holding Sessions, where industry experts guide you toward understanding your needs and achieving your goals.

- **Empowering Workshops:** Attend our workshops on "How to Master Digital Network Marketing," equipping you with the skills to excel in the digital realm.

- **Team Support:** Our dedicated team will stand by you as you journey toward increased income and success.

AURETICS SUPER INFINITY PLAN INSIGHTS are provided weekly, monthly, and daily. You will enjoy many consumer benefits, like:

- Retail Margin – up to 100% with Buy One Get One

- Cash Backs

- Monthly Offers

- 100% Satisfaction Money Back Guarantee

Extra Benefits:

- You will also avail various Lifestyle rewards

- Luxury Cars

- Luxury Homes

- You will also get a chance to work with SMART STRATEGIES (It's good to work hard, but better to work smart)

You will get to sell various innovative products that have a repeat demand of their own.

Also, the earning potential of AURETICS is POTENT:

Auretics Super Infinity Plan is extremely rewarding.

- In an average direct-selling company, you can expect an earning of Rs.6,000 after matching 25,000: 25,000 BV in both of your organisations.

- But in Auretics, if you work as directed by the company, then your payout can reach Rs.6,000 on a matching of 12,500: 12,500 BV.

- Not only that, if you work smartly, then matching only 8,000: 8,000 BV on both of your organisations can get you an earning of Rs.6,000 or more.

- How? It's simple. Our Super Bonus gives approx. 25% matching, i.e., Rs. 2,000.

- We have another income booster under the name of Rocket Income, that will give you: Rs.2000 x 2= Rs. 4,000

- **Total:** Rs. 6,000

Not only that, AURETICS will provide you with training on:

1. How to get quality leads

2. How to attract people

3. How to use Social Media to get the maximum crowd

4. How to make your community

5. How to create a team that will work for you

We will provide you with all the right TOOLS to perform these 7 steps:

1. CRM to Manage Your Contacts

2. Targeted Product Range

3. Right Marketing Message

4. Webinars will be regularly conducted by us

5. We will make a customised product page for your customers

6. We will give you an Online Platform where we handle complete back-end processes like Delivery of Goods, Customer Care, etc.

7. We will draft and send Follow-up messages to your customers.

Additional Benefits

1. In addition to all the benefits mentioned above, you also get a personal website from us.

2. And, to have you by our side, we will also give you a Personal Relationship Manager, who will work with you and help you reach your personal goals.

All of this is FREE OF COST.

Even our revised logistics are:

S. No.	Particulars	Cost
1.	Prepare Your Niche	-
2.	Gain Traffic	-
3.	Marketing Message	-
4.	Inviting for an Online Meeting/Webinar	-
5.	Sending Leads to Product's Landing Page	-
6.	Making the Sale	-
7.	Follow-ups for Re-order	-
	Total	**Nil**

The Time required to perform all these steps are:

S. No.	Particulars	Time
1.	Understanding the Needs of a Customer	Today
2.	Gain Traffic	
3.	Marketing Message	Today
4.	Inviting for an Online Meeting/Webinar	Today
5.	Sending Leads to Product's Landing Page	Today
6.	Making the Sale	Today
7.	Follow-ups for Re-order	Today
	Total	**Today**

And now, if you want to be a digital network marketer,

Contact: 8282828728

Not only that, but if you sign up for your valuable distributorship with us, your ID will be placed free of cost in our system. You will be free to place orders for the products you love the most.

However, if you activate your distributorship with more than 4,000BV of self-purchase of your own choice of products then we will give you all the above benefits, plus:

1. **Chalo Aur Paise Banaye Visual-Aid:**

   An ideal way to transform your prospects into a valued part of your team.

   Worth ~~Rs.2,000~~ **FREE**

2. **Auretics Super Infinity Compensation Plan:**

   Boost your team's growth and gain comprehensive insights into all the aspects of the Auretics Business.

   Worth ~~Rs.250~~ **FREE**

3. **The Seeds of 4x Success in 90 days workbook:**

   Fulfil all your dreams and discover the why behind your business journey.

   Worth ~~Rs.2,000~~ **FREE**

4. **7 Secrets that transform you from Mom to Mompreneur Book:**

   Simple Steps to Entrepreneurship.

   Worth ~~Rs.500~~ **FREE**

5. Distributor's Price List:

Worth ~~Rs.50~~ **FREE**

6. Auretics Product Book:

Worth ~~Rs.300~~ **FREE**

7. Control your sugar without eating any tablets, even when you don't want to exercise Visual-Aid:

The Ultimate Sugar Management Guide

Worth ~~Rs.2,000~~ **FREE**

8. A personalised Visiting Card with your name and mobile number:

Worth ~~Rs.499~~ **FREE**

9. Personalised ID card with your details:

Worth ~~Rs.299~~ **FREE**

10. Basic & Advanced Online Training:

Worth Rs.~~10,000~~ **FREE**

11. CRM & Billing Software:

Worth ~~Rs.10,000~~ **FREE**

The total benefits that you will get when you activate your distributorship with 4,000 BV is more than Rs.30,000.

Case Studies

We would like to show you some case studies of Individuals who joined our team and are now running a successful life.

***

I am a homemaker, and I joined Auretics because of passive income. When I saw the business plan, I felt secure because here both sides of business volumes are carried forward. The training & support system we have is amazing. Now, I can proudly say that I can fulfil my family's needs thanks to Auretics and the ASAR education system.

~Sushma Devi,
Rewari, Haryana

***

I always wanted to have my own income to ulfil my needs and my children's needs. I got this opportunity to work with Auretics Limited. Being a housewife, I worked from home and now can satisfy my needs as well as my children's needs. I have expanded my business to 7 different states from the comfort of my home. The best part of Auretics is they help women work digitally on social media. Now, I am making passive income.

~Shikha Saxena,
Gwalior, MP

I am a taxi driver. I was struggling to make money for my survival. So, I was looking for an opportunity where I could earn extra money. I got to know about Auretics Limited through social media. I believed in my seniors and started working. Now, I can make more money than my taxi income. I could expand my business in other states through social media. All credit goes to the Auretics system.

~Animesh Malo,
Kolkata, West Bengal

***

I have been part of the Auretics Family from the start, and I can generate a decent passive income that supports my dreams and also my family.

I have attended all the training, meetings, and seminars of the company, and I enjoy and share all the offers of the company too. The system is easy to follow, and I work mostly from my home.

Now, I can proudly say that I am financially independent on my terms, and I am sure that a lot of people are going to become diamonds in my network, and we all will succeed together as a team.

~Mrs. Rishita Yadav,
Palanpur, Gujarat

Call To Action

If you want to join us and have us by your side in your entrepreneurial journey, then Contact: + 91-8282828728

Or email us at **start@chaloaurpaisebanaye.com**

Lastly, stay Fit and active, and achieve success in Network Marketing by prioritising your well-being and wearing your winning smile.

START TODAY!

So, my dear friend, always remember:

1. If you want your dreams to come true, then wakeup.

2. Teach your people how to sponsor and teach.

3. You are not duplicating unless you are 3 levels deep.

4. The more you know, the slower you grow.

5. Real individuals don't ask for directions

6. Don't work hard for a living; work smart for a lifestyle.

7. The time for women is now.

8. One life, live it. One life, own it.